How Long Is It?

By Donna Loughran

Consultant
Linda Bullock
Math Curriculum Specialist

Children's Press®
A Division of Scholastic Inc.
New York   Toronto   London   Auckland   Sydney
Mexico City   New Delhi   Hong Kong
Danbury, Connecticut

Designer: Herman Adler Design
Photo Researcher: Caroline Anderson
The photo on the cover shows a child using a ruler to measure a line.

Library of Congress Cataloging–in–Publication Data

Loughran, Donna.
　How long is it? / by Donna Loughran.— 1st ed.
　　p. cm. — (Rookie read–about math)
　Includes bibliographical references and index.
　ISBN 0-516-24424-8 (lib. bdg.)　　　　0-516-24671-2 (pbk.)
　1. Length measurement—Juvenile literature. I. Title. II. Series.
QC102.L68 2004
530.8—dc22
　　　　　　　　　　　　　　2004005073

CHILDREN'S PRESS, and ROOKIE READ-ABOUT®,
and associated logos are trademarks and or registered trademarks
of Scholastic Library Publishing. SCHOLASTIC and associated logos
are trademarks and or registered trademarks of Scholastic Inc.

1 2 3 4 5 6 7 8 9 10 R 13 12 11 10 09 08 07 06 05 04

You can make small things.
You can make tall things.

4

You can measure those things in different ways.

There are different things to measure, too!

Long ago, people used their feet to measure the world. That didn't work very well.

Do you know why?

8

Not everyone's feet are the same size.

What could people do? They needed a tool to help them measure.

What tool helps people measure how long things are?

A ruler. Who decided how long a ruler is?

12

A ruler is also another name for a king or queen.

Maybe long ago, someone made a tool as long as a king's foot. The person called the tool a ruler, like the king.

People used the first
ruler to make more rulers.

People everywhere began
to use rulers to measure
how long things were.

Today, many people in the
United States use rulers
like these.

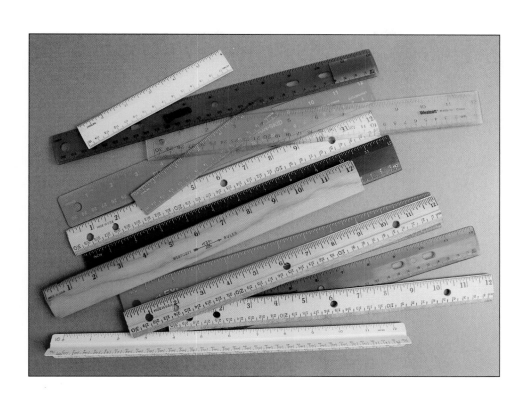

15

16

What if you didn't have a ruler? You could make up your own way to measure.

Look at these butterflies. Which butterfly is bigger?

One is three crayons long. The other one is two crayons long.

Now, try using a ruler.
A ruler is 1 foot long.

Look around you. Find
something that is 1 foot
long. Measure it to be sure.

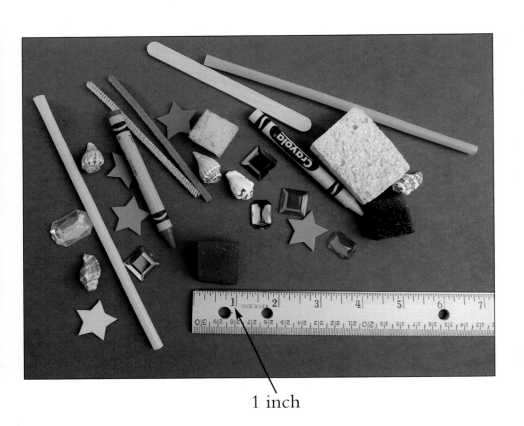

1 inch

Did you find things shorter than 1 foot long? You can measure these things, too.

A ruler is divided into 12 equal parts. Each part is called an inch.

Find something that is 1 inch long.

A pushpin is about 1 inch long. A large paper clip is about 2 inches long.

How long is your favorite crayon?

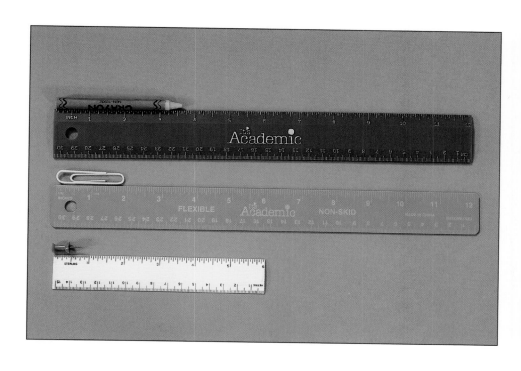

23

1/2 inch

24

Sometimes, things are smaller than an inch. You can measure them, too.

Each inch is divided into parts. The metal part on this pencil is about 1/2 inch long.

Sometimes, things are longer than a foot.

A baseball bat is about 3 feet long. Three feet make a yard.

You can use a yardstick to measure yards.

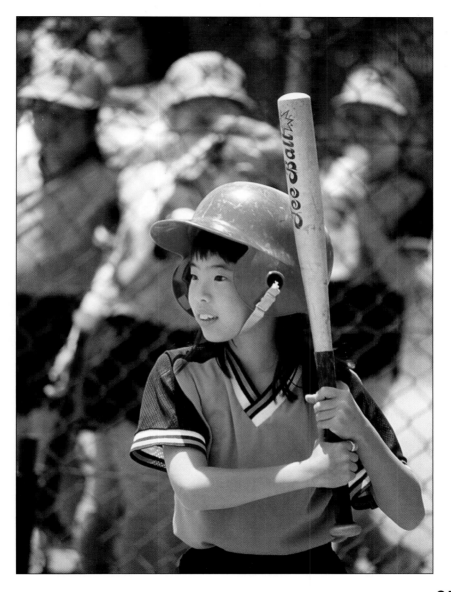

These boys are using a
yardstick to measure a door.

Look around you. What
will you measure?

Words You Know

feet

foot

inch

measure

rulers

31

Index

About the Author

Donna Loughran is a writer, editor, artist, and multimedia instructional designer.

Photo Credits

Photographs © 2004: Ellen B. Senisi: cover, 3, 4, 11, 15, 16, 19, 20, 23, 24, 29, 30 top right, 30 bottom, 31 bottom, 31 top; PhotoEdit/David Young-Wolff: 7, 27; PictureQuest/BananaStock, Ltd: 8, 30 top left; The Art Archive/Picture Desk/Dagli Orti/Rosenborg Castle Copenhagen: 12.